REASONS

FOR ABANDONING THE THEORY OF

FREE TRADE,

AND

ADOPTING THE PRINCIPLE OF

PROTECTION TO AMERICAN INDUSTRY.

Addressed to the Farmers and Working Men of the United States.

BY

WILLIAM D. KELLEY, M. C.

REPRINTED FROM THE AUTHOR'S "SPEECHES, ADDRESSES AND LETTERS ON INDUSTRIAL AND FINANCIAL QUESTIONS."

PHILADELPHIA:
HENRY CAREY BAIRD,
INDUSTRIAL PUBLISHER,
406 WALNUT STREET.
1872.

REASONS

FOR ABANDONING THE THEORY OF

FREE TRADE,

AND

ADOPTING THE PRINCIPLE OF

PROTECTION TO AMERICAN INDUSTRY.

Addressed to the Farmers and Working Men of the United States.

BY

WILLIAM D. KELLEY, M. C.

REPRINTED FROM THE AUTHOR'S "SPEECHES, ADDRESSES AND LETTERS ON INDUSTRIAL AND FINANCIAL QUESTIONS."

PHILADELPHIA:
HENRY CAREY BAIRD,
INDUSTRIAL PUBLISHER,
406 WALNUT STREET.
1872.

REASONS FOR ABANDONING THE

THEORY OF FREE TRADE.*

IN offering this volume to the public it is proper to state that I make no pretension to a critical knowledge of literature or rhetoric, and that, when preparing the papers it contains, I did not suppose they would ever be collected for republication. They are expressions of opinion called forth by occasions; and, as the reader will observe, not unfrequently in the excitement of current debate in the National House of Representatives, or in response to invitations to address popular assemblies under circumstances that precluded the possibility of reducing them to writing in advance of their delivery. It is proper also to say that I am not wholly responsible for their publication in book form, inasmuch as they have been collected and annotated in deference to the judgment and wishes of citizens of different sections of the country, who, though strangers to each other and engaged in pursuits involving apparently conflicting interests, agreed in persuading me that by this labor I might render a service to those of my countrymen who are engaged in farming or who depend on their labor for the means of supporting their children while giving them that measure of education without which no American citizen should be permitted to attain maturity.

While I regret some expressions in the colloquial portions of the Congressional speeches, and would have omitted them could it have been done without impairing the argument, I find no reason to question the soundness of my positions. The theory that labor—the productive exercise of the skill and muscular power of men who are responsible for the faithful and intelligent performance of civic and other duties—is merely a raw material, and that that nation which pays least for it is wisest and best governed, is inadmissible in a democracy; and when we shall determine to starve the bodies and minds of our operatives in order that we may successfully compete in common markets with the productions of the under-paid and poorly-fed peasants of Europe and the paupers of England, we shall assail the foundations of a govern-

* This originally appeared as the Introduction to "Speeches, Addresses, and Letters on Industrial and Financial Questions."

ment which rests upon the intelligence and integrity of its people. To defend our country against this result, is the office of a protective tariff, and for this duty it alone is sufficient.

This was not always my belief. My youthful judgment was captivated by the plausible but sophistical generalities by which cosmopolitanism or free trade is advocated, and my faith in them remained unshaken till events involving the prostration of our domestic industry, and the credit not only of cities and States, but of the nation, demonstrated the insufficiency or falsity of my long and dearly cherished theories. In 1847, I had seen with gratification the protective tariff of 1842 succeeded by the revenue or free trade tariff of 1846. To promote this change, I had labored not only with zeal and industry, but with undoubting faith that experience would prove its beneficence. A number of remarkable circumstances conspired to promote the success of the experiment. The potato rot was creating an unprecedented foreign demand for our breadstuffs. It was then ravaging the fields of England and the continent, having already devastated the fields, and more than decimated the people of Ireland, who, to escape starvation, were fleeing *en masse* to this country. The gold fields of Australia and California had just been discovered, and promised, by increasing the circulating medium of the world, and concentrating many thousands of emigrants, who would engage in mining, in countries without agriculture or manufactures, to create great markets for our productions of every kind, thus increasing our trade and quickening every department of industry. Beyond all this, however, and, as I afterwards came to understand, as a result of the condemned protective tariff, in conjunction with recent improvements in our naval architecture, our commercial marine was growing rapidly, our ship builders were prosperous, and our ship owners were receiving as compensation for extra speed a shilling a chest in advance of English freights for carrying tea from Hong Kong or Canton to London. Each of these circumstances was a good augury for the success of a tariff for revenue only. Going into effect under such favorable conditions, it must, I believed, procure for our farmers cheap foreign fabrics and wares, and secure a constantly increasing market for the productions of their farms; and by enlarging our share in the carrying trade of the world compel the rapid construction of ships and steamers, whose employment would increase our receipts of coin and immigrants. Trade being so nearly free, we must in a few years see the ships of all nations coming to New York for assorted cargoes, and our commercial metropolis would then become the financial centre of the world, in which international balances would be settled. That these were but a small part of the great results my theories promised will appear to any one who will refer to the annual reports of the then Secretary of the Treasury, Robert J. Walker, who was not more sanguine than I, and whose statements of the general prosperity that would flow from a revenue tariff were as positive and rose-tinted as those with which Messrs. Atkinson and Wells now beguile their followers.

Were we early revenue reformers worshippers at false shrines, or did the sequel approve our faith? History answers these questions with emphasis. It needed but a decade to demonstrate the folly of attempting to create a market for our increasing agricultural productions, and to develop our mining and manufacturing resources by the application of the beautiful abstractions disseminated by Free Trade Leagues. It was just ten years after the substitution of the revenue tariff of 1846 for the protective tariff of 1842, that the general bankruptcy of the American people was announced by the almost simultaneous failure of the Ohio Life and Trust Company, and the Bank of Pennsylvania, and the suspension of specie payments by almost every bank in the country. In that brief period, our steamers had been supplanted by foreign lines, and our clipper ships driven from the sea, or restricted to carrying between our Atlantic and Pacific ports. At the close of that brief term, the ship-yards of Maine were almost as idle as they are now when railroads traverse the country in all directions and compete with ships in carrying even such bulky commodities as sugar, cotton, and leaf tobacco;* and while the families of thousands of unemployed workmen in our great cities were in want of food, Illinois farmers found in corn, for which there was no market, the cheapest fuel they could obtain, though their fields were underlaid by an inexhaustible deposit of coal that is almost co-extensive with the State. Capital invested in factories, furnaces, forges, rolling mills and machinery was idle and unproductive, and there was but a limited home market for cotton or wool. Taking advantage of this condition of affairs, foreign dealers put their prices down sufficiently to bankrupt the cotton States, to induce many of our farmers to give up sheep raising, and to constrain many thousand immigrants who could not find employment to return to their native countries. 1847 had been a good year for farmers, mechanics, miners and merchants; but 1857 was a good year for sheriffs,

* See figures from the report of Mr. Nimmo, Chief of Tonnage Division, in note, page 431.

constables and marshals, though few were purchasers at their sales except mortgagees, judgment creditors, and capitalists who were able to pay cash at nominal prices for unproductive establishments, and hold them till happier circumstances should restore their value.

Not one of the glowing predictions of Political Economy had been fulfilled, and the surprise with which I contemplated the contrast presented by the condition of the country with what it had been at the close of the last period of protection, amounted to amazement. Nor did my cherished theories enable me to ascertain the cause of the sudden and general paralysis, or suggest a remedy for it. Yet I could not abandon them, for, as their ablest recent American champion, Mr. Edward Atkinson, of Boston, in his article in the *Atlantic Monthly* for October, says of the details of the Revenue Reform budget, they were "simple, sensible, and right." Was not each one a truism that might be expressed as a maxim—an indisputable proposition—the mere statement of which established its verity? To prove that they were not responsible for the prostration of our industries, the want of a market for our breadstuffs, and the widespread bankruptcy that prevailed, required the enunciation of but one of them: CUSTOMS DUTIES ARE TAXES.* No one can dispute this proposition, for the people pay them, and the Government collects them, and not only may but should raise its entire revenue through them. Surely nobody could have the temerity to assert that an industrious and prosperous people could be reduced to idleness and bankruptcy by the repeal or reduction of taxes, and thus charge this national disaster to free trade and the *doctrinaires* who had kindly taught us Political Economy, and induced us to abandon the protective system. The case was clear. Yet, strange to say, perfect as the demonstration seemed to be, I was forced by the condition of the country to doubt and ask myself whether, in some occult way, the reduction of the rate of duties might not have had something to do with producing it. The results promised by the teachers of my cherished science, and those attained by experiment, were irreconcilable, and I was constrained to ask myself whether it might not be possible that Political Economy was not an exact—an absolute—science, the laws of which were equally applicable to all nations, without regard to the conditions and requirements of the people, or the extent, variety or degree of the development of their resources? It was easier to harbor this doubt than to believe the alternative, which was, that the Almighty had not put

* See Dr. Bushnell, in note, pages 317, 318.

production, commerce and trade in the United States under the government of universal and immutable laws, but had left them to the control of chance. This conclusion being inadmissible, there was nothing left but to waive the further consideration of the subject, or to withdraw my theories from the dazzling light of abstract reason, and examine them under the shade of present experience.

It is a cardinal maxim among the adherents of free trade that TWO MARKETS IN WHICH TO BUY AND SELL ARE BETTER THAN ONE, and I could not dispute it; but when in the progress of my re-examination, I announced it to an intelligent protectionist as indisputable, he admitted that it was so. "But," said he, "where is the evidence that free trade is the road to two markets for the United States?" In endeavoring to answer this question satisfactorily to myself it became apparent that I had evaded the real point at issue. Both parties to the controversy agree that two markets are better than one. But the protectionists say, "Do not risk the loss or diminution of the home market afforded by our people when fully employed and well paid, by attempting to secure another, in a direction where success will be, to say the least, exceedingly doubtful;" the free traders saying, "Court foreign trade by all means, and as you are sure of the home market, you will thus secure two." Which are right? To determine this, we must ascertain whether trade between nations is reciprocal or nearly so.* To settle this question, I made a thorough and searching appeal to the trade statistics of our own and other countries, and ascertained that the amount of our productions consumed by the manufacturing nations of Europe has in no degree, in any year, depended upon the amount of their productions consumed by us; but on the contrary, that they never took an equal amount, and frequently, when we were taking most from them, took least of everything but cotton, which they could not obtain elsewhere, from us. Thus it had often occurred that when our store-houses were being gorged with productions of the underpaid workmen of England, she, taking gold and silver from us, had gone to Prussia, Germany, Austria, Turkey, and France, who bought but little from her, and the chief diet of whose laboring people consisted of rye bread, potatoes and garlic, for her breadstuffs. This examination further showed that the amount of breadstuffs England will ever take from us is measured by the slight deficiency she may expect to experience after having exhausted the markets of those lower priced

---

* See extract from Kirk's Social Politics, in note, page 186.

countries, whose people are subjects, and whose wages mark the minimum on which families may subsist. When Æsop's stupid dog snapped at the shadow in the water he lost his bone; and the investigation convinced me that the attempt to secure a second market by reducing our customs duties had destroyed our home market, but opened no other for any of our productions except gold and silver, and State and corporate bonds. It had given England, with her low rates of wages and interest, two markets in which to sell, and by destroying our home market for grain, an additional one in which to buy; but had deprived us of the one on which, under an adequate system of protection, we could always depend, as has been shown by the uniform general prosperity that has prevailed since the Morrill tariff of 1861 went into effect. Thus it appeared that the fallacy was not in the abstract proposition which neither party disputed, but in the assumption that free trade would insure us two markets.

Kindred to the foregoing proposition, and equally undeniable as an abstract truth, seemed this other: YOU SHOULD BUY WHERE YOU CAN BUY CHEAPEST.* Yet we had been doing this for ten years, and were bankrupt. This condition of affairs could not, it seemed to me, be the result of reduced rates of duties, and the payment of reduced prices for what we had consumed. What process of reasoning could show these facts to be related as cause and effect? England could sell us railroad bars to lay over our wide stretches of limestone country, and our immense fields of coal and iron, at lower prices than, in the undeveloped condition of our resources, and with our higher priced labor and money, we could produce them; and we had bought our supply from her. With her accumulated capital, machinery, skilled labor, and her lower wages, she could also spin and weave cotton and wool, and make the cloth into garments cheaper than our countrymen could, and we had bought from her our clothes, or the cloth from which to cut them. So, too, she could sell us chemicals, prepared drugs, pig-iron, raw steel, and an immense number of other commodities for less money than we could produce them; and we had gone to her markets and bought them where we could buy them cheapest. Meanwhile, we had mined hundreds of millions of dollars worth of gold and silver; had raised unprecedented crops of cotton, tobacco, and breadstuffs; had produced immense supplies of naval stores and other exportable commodities; and had, withal, issued hundreds of millions of interest-bearing bonds, by which our future productions and those of our posterity

---

* See Dr. Bushnell, in notes, pages 285 and 354.

were mortgaged. Yet, strange to tell, in spite of the lower duties paid on our imports, and the lower than American prices at which we had procured our supplies, we had not gold and silver enough to serve as a basis for a redeemable currency, and being, in many instances, unable to pay the interest on our bonds were sued and sold out by our English friends, to whom our gold, silver, and bonds had gone. We were, however, rich in one class of commodities—the productions of the farm. Of these the people of the Western States had a superabundance. It was, however, unfortunately, not possible to make them available, as our English creditors would not take them even in payment of debts unless we would, after paying for their transportation to the sea-board, let them have them at the low prices at which they could obtain like articles which had been produced by the ill-fed peasants of Russia, Prussia, Austria, Hungary, and Turkey. Than to do this it was better for farmers in the extreme West to let their crops perish on the field.

Our condition was anomalous. There was no element of wealth, or of the conveniences of life that could be produced by a reasonable amount of labor outside of the tropics of which we did not possess greater stores in the form of raw materials than any other nation; and of the productions of the farm our supply was so superabundant that some of us were, as I have said, using corn for fuel; yet, our manufacturing operatives were poor and unemployed, our farmers were unable to pay for past purchases or fresh supplies, and our merchants and banks, involved in the common fate, were unable to meet their obligations. Did this strange experience prove that it is not best to buy where you can buy cheapest? No. But it did prove that money-price is not the test of cheapness; and that we buy more cheaply, though the nominal price of each commodity be higher when we buy what we consume of those who will buy what we produce at fair prices, than we do when we buy at lower prices for cash, or on credit, and permit our productions to perish for the want of a market. Thus did deductions from unquestionable and present experience demonstrate the fallacy of the system of "established principles," which I had cherished as a sufficient economic creed.

The terrible ordeal through which the working classes of England are now passing, is constraining her statesmen and scholars to bring the prevailing system of Political Economy to the test of experience, and one of these scholars has been bold enough to deny not only the policy, but the morality of the proposition I have just considered. Mr. David Syme, in a well-considered and powerful article on the "Method of Po-

litical Economy,' in the *Westminster Review* for July, 1871, which has come under my notice since the foregoing was written, says:

"A close investigation will, indeed, lead to the conclusion that the spirit of the moral law is incompatible with the modern economic doctrine of buying in the cheapest, and selling in the dearest market. For a scrupulous sense of duty will often compel a man to act contrary to his own personal interests. Such a man will conduct himself in his business relations on the strictest principles of honor and fair dealing. He will refuse to take an advantage when the law may permit it, when, by so doing, he might prejudice the interests of others. He will not take all he can get, and give as little as he can; but he will give as much as he can afford, and take only what is fair and equitable. This is not Utopianism, but the true spirit of the moral law.

"If, moreover, we consider man in the social state, we shall find that the individual is bound to recognize the interests of others as well as his own. He cannot, even if he would, be guided in his social relations by an exclusive regard for his own interests. In seeking his own advantage he must be careful to do nothing that might in any way be injurious to his neighbor. He must not sell a spurious article for a genuine one, nor a deleterious compound for a wholesome one. He must not use false labels or unjust weights. . . . . Economic science recognizes the existence of the social state, and the social state presupposes the existence of the social virtues—honor, honesty, and a regard for the feelings and rights of others."

It was not easy to abandon opinions I had cherished through so many years, and in which my faith had been so implicit, but it was still more difficult to accept the opposite system, that of protection, which I had so often denounced as false, selfish, and exclusive. Nor did I do this hastily: more than two years had been devoted to the writings of the ablest advocates of both systems, and still I halted between them. Meanwhile, it became apparent to me, not only that Political Economy was not a science, but that it was impossible to frame a system of abstract economic propositions which would be universally applicable and beneficent; and, further, that the same principles could not be applied beneficially to England and the United States. The conditions of the two nations are not the same, but are in striking contrast. England is a small island, but the United States embraces almost the entire available territory of a continent. The former is burdened by an excess of population, and vexed by the question as to how she shall dispose of the excess; but our great need is industrious people, and with us the question is how can we increase immigration. She has to import food for half her people, and her foreign trade is to her what seed-time and harvest are to the countries from which she procures the breadstuffs she requires but cannot produce; but were they on our soil, we could feed ten times the number of her whole people; and even while I write, the merchants of Minnesota, Iowa, and other northwestern States are suffering financial embarrassment because the farmers they supply cannot find a market for their crops. She is dependent on foreign countries for most of the raw materials she consumes; but we have within our limits exhaustless stores of every variety not dependent upon tropical heat for their production. Her resources are ascertained and developed; but ours await development, and in regions, any one of which is larger than all western Europe, including the British Islands, await definite ascertainment. Her population is compacted within narrow limits, and her railroads are completed and paid for; but our people are settled sparsely over half a continent, and most of our system of roads, for which the capital is yet to be produced, is to be constructed. The charges for transportation within her circumscribed and populous limits are very light; but over our extended and thinly-settled country they are necessarily heavy. Her factories were erected and supplied with machinery while she maintained the most rigid system of protection the world has ever seen; but ours are to be built as experiments in the face of threatened free trade which would involve a more unequal competition than any against which she defended hers by protective duties and absolute prohibitions. Her average rate of interest is 3 per cent. per annum; but ours is never less than 6 per cent. per annum, and in large sections of the country is often 3 percent. per month. The great body of her laborers, even since the recent extension of the suffrage, are *subjects* without civic duties; but ours are *citizens*, and liable to such duties. She pays the daily wages of her workmen with shillings; but we pay ours with dollars worth four shillings each, and give many classes of them more dollars than she does shillings: It is, therefore, impossible that the same economic polity can be applied with equal advantage to countries whose condition presents so many and such important contrasts.

Ten years under a tariff which levied the lowest rates of duties consistent with the purpose of raising by imports the amount of revenue required by the current expenses of the government, sufficed to destroy the industries and credit of the American people. The immense advantages England possesses in manufactures and trade have enabled her to withstand the untoward influence of free trade for a longer period than we were able to; but at the end of a quarter of a century it has become apparent that even the mistress of the seas and the work-shop of the world cannot, at less cost than the loss of national prestige and threatened revolution, throw her ports open to unrestricted competition. The effect on England of the abandonment of the protective system does not exhibit itself in wide-spread bankruptcy as it did with us. The enormous accumulations of capital held by her privileged classes have prevented this. It is, however, observable in the disappearance of the small farmer, and of the small work-shop that in more prosperous times would have expanded into a factory; in the concentration of land and machinery in the hands of a constantly diminishing number of persons; and in the rapidly increasing destitution, idleness, intemperance, and despair of her laboring classes.*

In the course of his admirable sermon before the University of Oxford, December 20th, 1868, Rev. Brooke Lambert said: "The severance between the rich and the poor is to me an even sadder thing than the wretched state of the labor market. I can fancy a remedy possible for the one, I can foresee no remedy for the other. The gap between them seems widening every day, as trade and land fall into the hands of large capitalists, who absorb all smaller concerns, all smaller holdings." And *Blackwood's Magazine* for April, 1870, in an article entitled "The State, the Poor, and the Country," says: "The lamentable depression of trade, and consequent want of employment which have recently prevailed, have now reached a most serious magnitude in many of the larger towns, and most of all in London and its far-spreading suburbs. The intensity of the distress in the metropolitan districts has not been equalled in recent times. And the break-down of our Poor-law system, despite all efforts of voluntary associations, has been appalling in its results. Not a week passes without several cases of 'deaths from starvation,' duly attested by the verdict of coroners' inquests, where the medical and other evidence reveals an amount of unaided wretchedness and starvation, which one would suppose impossible in a civilized country. Men, women and children dying from sheer famine in the heart of the wealthiest city in the world!"

The extracts from the works of Sir John Byles, Sir Edward Sullivan, Professor Kirk, Messrs. Grant, Patterson, Smith, Hoyle, and other recent British writers, which will be found in notes throughout this volume, more than con-

* See extracts, Appendix, pp. 29–32.

firm this statement. Sir Edward Sullivan admonishes the governing classes that if they do not wish to reduce England to the condition of a manufacturing country without workshops or skilled workmen, they must protect native industry sufficiently to restore the home market for cotton fabrics, which has fallen off 35 per cent., by reason of the fact that the enforced idleness of masses of the working people has deprived them of the ability to consume this indispensable element of comfortable attire; and Mr. Hoyle produces from official statistics the figures to prove the startling statement.

Nor can the British Government longer close its eyes to this distress and continue to assert that THE LAW OF SUPPLY AND DEMAND is the heaven-appointed and all-sufficient regulator of societary movements. It is even now feebly attempting to regulate both supply and demand by its own action. To this end Earl Granville, Foreign Secretary, as early as the 14th of April, 1870, addressed a circular dispatch to the Governors of British Colonies, from which I take the following paragraph:

"The distress prevailing among the laboring classes in many parts of the United Kingdom has directed public attention to the question of Emigration as a means of relief. It has been urged on Her Majesty's Government that while there are in this country large numbers of well-conducted, industrious laborers, for whom no employment can be found, there exists in most of the colonies a more extensive demand for labor than the laboring class on the spot can supply. The result of emigration would, therefore, it is said, be equally advantageous to the emigrant and the colonies—to the former, by placing him in a position to earn an independence; to the latter, by supplying a want that retards their progress and prosperity. Under the circumstances, Her Majesty's Government is anxious to be furnished with your opinion as to the prospects which the colony under your government holds out to emigrants, both of the agricultural and the artisan class.

. . . .

"The points on which we should be specially desirous of receiving information are: the classes of laborers whose labor is most in demand in the colony under your government; the numbers for whom employment could be found; the probable wages they would earn; whether married men with families could obtain wages to enable them to support their families, and house accommodation for their shelter; what assistance or facilities would be provided to pass the emigrants to the districts where their labor is in demand; and whether any pecuniary assistance would be granted either toward their passages, or toward providing depots and subsistence on their first arrival, or toward sending them up to the country."

That England will soon so far modify her revenue system as to re-adopt many of the distinctive features of the Protective System, I confidently predict. Not that I credit her privileged classes with quick or enlarged sympathy with the laboring classes, but because I know that they have always had sufficient tact to avert popular outbreak by timely concession. And though I remember how the people of Ireland and Orissa were permitted to starve, I still believe that the consumers of England will consent to pay duties on such goods as compete with English labor in the home market, and relieve from taxation the tea, coffee, sugar, currants, raisins, tobacco, and spirits of the laboring classes, rather than incur the risk of widespread famine in London, Lancashire, and other great industrial centres of the country. But, were they capable of the fatuity of withholding their consent, the question has passed from their decision. Their last concession to the popular will, the extension of the suffrage, makes this one inevitable. The article in *Blackwood*, already referred to, thus defines the position of the question:

"A new power has been introduced into our political system, new forces are at work within the pale of the Constitution. The Government has become National in the fullest sense of the word; and with the change a new breath of life is stirring society. New views are rapidly forming; new hopes and aspirations are entering into the heart of the masses. The rule of the middle classes established by the Reform Bill of 1832, has come to an end; and the doctrines which regulated the legislation of that period are now being tested and considered from a different, indeed opposite point of view.

"For nearly forty years the prime object of our legislation has been the interests of the Consumers; *now*, we shall soon have the masses advocating their own interests as Producers. What is more, the State has now become simply the nation itself, acting through a chosen body of administrators; and it is easy to discern that under the new *régime* the Government will be called upon to adopt a very different policy in domestic affairs from that represented by the principle of the Whigs and *doctrinaires*, which has been paramount since 1832. That principle well suited the interests of the wealthy and comparatively fortunate classes, who needed no help from the State, yet who got all they asked for, by the abolition of all custom duties which shackled their business. But will that principle keep its ground now that the weaker classes also have a voice in the Government?

Will they not maintain that they, as an integral part of the nation, have a claim to be fully considered in the policy of the Government; and that, if they can point out any system of governmental action which will benefit them, without doing injustice to the rest of the community, no *doctrinaire* limitations upon the actions of the State shall be allowed to stand in the way? The maxims of the Liberals, which have been predominant since 1832, will be thrown into the crucible and tried anew. Already in vague murmurs, which ere long will become distinct and earnest speech, the masses are beginning to say that the principles which have been in vogue during the rule of the middle classes will not suit them. 'Our interests,' they say, 'are those of Producers, not of Consumers.

"'We also are poor, and you are wealthy; we are weak, and you are strong; with us employment is a far more precarious thing than it is with you, and we have but small earnings to fall back upon when out of work. State help, though not needful to the middle classes, is needed at times by us; and we shall never rest contented until that principle is acknowledged and properly applied.'"

The government cannot long refuse to listen to this demand, which no longer comes from the laboring classes alone, but is enforced by many such writers as those to whom I am indebted for many of my most instructive notes, and now by *Blackwood*, the *Quarterly Reviews*, and other great organs of opinion. That school of political economists who propound free trade as the result of their system is finding less favor with the thinkers of England than heretofore. They discover that it is not producing the results it promised, but other and very different ones, and are demanding that it be tested by the inductive system, and proven by the facts of experience. It has become clear to many of them that under its influence the working people are not prosperous or contented; that the home market for some of their great staples diminishes steadily; and that in spite of Government assurances that British trade increases, it is stationary, if not absolutely diminishing. Discarding statements prepared by skilful statistical jugglers like Mr. Wells, our late Commissioner of Revenue, they are comparing and analyzing results for themselves, and have thus detected the fraudulent practices by which they have been deceived. The last trick British statistics have been made to play was by her Majesty's Commissioners of Customs, who, to prove the steady increase of trade, proclaimed with much triumph that the exports during 1870 were 11 per cent. greater than they were in 1868. This cheering result, which, isolated from the general facts to which it is related, is true, is made to prove the steady increase of trade by a device that would do no discredit to the cunning and audacity of our great statistical manipulator. This is the process by which it is done. The French army moved toward the German frontier about the 15th of July, 1870, and at the close of the year the war was at its height, promising not only to be of long duration, but threatening to involve all Europe. It caused a general suspension of the industries of France and Germany, whose wares and fabrics were crowding those of England out of so many markets, or the employment of their operatives in the production of arms and munitions of war. It also gave England an immense market for these. But what was, perhaps, more important than all this, it caused the withdrawal of the commercial marine of those countries from the ocean, and gave the ships and shops of England a monopoly of the carrying and foreign trade of the world. Her trade could not fail to be exceptionally large that year, as owing to the war having extended far into it, and been prolonged by the folly of the *Commune* it will be this year. The Commissioners of Customs prove the virtues of free trade by contrasting the exports of this exceptional year with those of 1868, in which they were lower than they have been since 1865. The following official figures will suffice to show that the exports from Great Britain for the last four years, including 1870, which was so exceptionally large, have on the average been less than during 1866 by the considerable sum of more than $6,700,000 per annum:

1866.	Total value of British Exports................	£188,917,536
1867.	" " "	181,183,971
1868.	" " "	179,463,644
1869.	" " "	189,953,957
1870.	" " "	199,649,938

The reader who will add the value of the four years, '67–70, and divide the result by four, and compare the figures thus obtained with the total exports of 1866, will ascertain precisely how rapidly and steadily the trade of Great Britain increases.

Mr. Syme, in the course of his article in the *Westminster Review*, to which I have referred, says: "Political Economy exhibits no sign of progressiveness. Instead of discoveries, of which we have had none of any consequence since Adam Smith's time, we have had endless disputation and setting up of dogmas. Whatever progress may have been made in other sciences during the last century, there has been none in this. The most elementary principles are still matters of dispute. The doctrine of free trade, for instance, which is looked upon as the crowning triumph of Political Economy, is still very far from being universally recognized. Even in England, after twenty years' trial under most favorable circumstances, free trade has been put upon its defence. We make no progress, and from the very nature of our method of investigation, we can make none. The Political Economist observes phenomena with a foregone conclusion as to their cause. His method, in fact, is the method of the savage. The phenomena of nature, the thunder, the lightning, or the earthquake, strike the savage with awe and wonder; but he only looks within himself for an explanation of these phenomena. To him, therefore, the forces of nature are only the efforts of beings like himself, great and powerful, no doubt, but with good and evil propensities, and subject to every human caprice. Like the Political Economist, he works within the vicious circle of his own feelings, and he cannot comprehend, any more than the savage, how he can discover the laws which regulate the phenomena which he sees around him. The savage would reduce the Divine mind to the dimensions of the human; the Political Economist would reduce the human mind to the dimensions of his ideal.

"Our conclusion is, that the inductive method is alone applicable to the investigation of economic science, and that we shall never be able to make any solid progress so long as we continue to follow the *à priori* method—a method which has not aided, but clogged and fettered us in the pursuit of truth, and which is utterly alien to the spirit of modern scientific inquiry."

For the edification of those who may be incredulous as to free trade being on its defence in England, Mr. Syme refers to Professor Bonamy Price's arraignment of it in the *Contemporary Review* of February, 1871.*

The *London Quarterly Review* for July [1871], contains a spirited article on "Economical Fallacies and Labor Utopias," in which it handles with great freedom "the school of political economists now in the ascendant." The date at which it was published proves that the author could not have seen the article entitled "Free Trade—Revenue Reform," in our *Atlantic* for October, yet he says: "There is an utopianism which counts its chickens before they are hatched, nay, cackles over chickens it expects to hatch from eggs that are addled." Referring to Mr. John Stuart Mill, who, had the *Atlantic's* article been anonymous, might, from the freedom with which it disposes of existing relations and interests, well have been suspected of its authorship, the *Quarterly* proceeds to say:

"If Mr. Mill, the recognized leader of that school, is to be designated as an economical 'enthusiast,' or perhaps more

* See also remarks of Sir John Byles and Mr. R. H. Patterson, in notes, pages 199 and 200; and also of Sir Edward Sullivan, in note, pages 378, 379.

properly as the founder and propagator o. economical enthusiasm, he has earned that designation more by the excessive exercise of the dialectical than of the imaginative faculty, and does not so much body forth to himself the forms of things unknown, as suggest to his disciples revolutions, unrealized even in imagination, of all existing relations between classes and sexes, as *logically* admissible, and not to be set aside as practically chimerical without actual experiment. His enthusiasm is the speculative passion of starting ever fresh game in the wide field of abstract social possibilities—philosophically indifferent to all objections drawn from the actual conditions of men, women, or things in the concrete. Mr. Mill would be very capable, like Condorcet, of deriving from the doctrine of human perfectibility the inference that there was no demonstrable reason why the duration of human life might not be prolonged indefinitely by discoveries (hereafter to be made) in hygiene. And to all objections drawn from universal human experience of the growth and decay of vital power within a limited period, it would be quite in the character of his mind and temper to reply calmly that the life of man, like the genius of woman, had not hitherto been developed under such conditions as to draw out its capabilities to the full extent. Like Condorcet, too, while dealing perturbation all around him, Mr. Mill is imperturbable, and might be described as *he* was, as '*un mouton en rage—un Volcan couvert de neige!*' "

It was the opinion of the great Bonaparte, that Political Economy would grind empires to powder, though they were made of adamant. The British Government is proving the excellence of his judgment, and schoolmen and theorists are industriously laboring to induce the American people to confirm it by even a grander illustration. This pretended science which, Mr. Mill says, "necessarily reasons from assumptions, and not from facts," is sedulously and devoutly taught at Yale, and most of our leading colleges. It is fortunate that the intimate relations of many of the students with the industries and people of the country render the scholasticisms of their teachers harmless; and in parting from them, they sometimes throw back upon them the terrible results of experience, as their reply to the weary chapters of deductions from assumptions with which they have been tortured. How boldly and aptly, yet respectfully this may be done, was shown by Mr. Orville Justus Bliss, of Chicago, at Yale's last commencement. A leading scholar of his class, he had been selected to deliver the Valedictory, in the course of which he said:

"A cry for relief has gone forth, and refuses to be hushed.

We cannot always ignore these men. Neither can we forever satisfy them by quoting Adam Smith. Suppose some wise individual should stand with a copy of 'The Wealth of Nations' in his hand before a mob of London bread-rioters, and begin to read the chapter on wages; would they all go off rejoicing in the beauties of the science, and convinced that they were happy? Political Economy has had ample trial in England. A mill agent recently said, 'I regard my work people just as I regard my machinery. So long as they can do my work for what I choose to pay them, I keep them, getting out of them all I can. When my machines get old and useless, I reject them, and get new; and these people are part of my machinery.' Is not that a sufficiently rigorous application of the law of demand and supply? And it describes the whole factory system in England, up to the time when the agitators took it in hand. What it has done for England, I need not repeat. Suffice it to say, that Political Economy, as a solution of this question, is a disastrous failure."

And again: "The poor cannot help themselves. They are tied hand and foot with an enslaving destitution. We say: 'It is a free country; let every one make of himself as much as he can.' We challenge one and all to an unbounded competition. But to these people the seeming fairness is mockery. It rivals the brave boy who first takes a good long start, and then turns around and offers to race with you to the next corner. The child of the laborer may lift himself from his degradation, and become a power for good. But there must be some measure of intelligence, to serve as a basis upon which to build. They must be made to feel that society is their friend, not an enemy, whose prosperity is their defeat. What, then, is the laying of a cable, or the spanning of a continent? What beauty do they find in literature, what exaltation in science—I had almost said, what solace in religion? Not in the name of an endangered society, imminent as its peril is; not in the interests of great money-wielders, plainly as those interests point to educated labor, do I plead the cause of these people; but because they are part of our common humanity, and have a right to partake of our common, intellectual, æsthetic, and social delight."

I have said that I believe England will soon readopt many of the distinctive principles of the protective system. Unless *we* determine otherwise, she must do this soon. Her newly enfranchised producers will demand it, and the action of her colonies will impart vehemence to the demand. Protection is a settled principle with the governments of Victoria, New South Wales, Queensland, and other Australian colonies. Speaking of this, together with the fact that they are establishing Customs Unions on the principle of the Zollverein, Charles Wentworth Dilke, in his *Greater Britain*, says: "It is a common doctrine in the colonies of England that a nation cannot be called 'independent' if it has to cry out to another for supplies of necessaries; that true national existence is first attained when the country becomes capable of supplying to its own citizens those goods without which they cannot exist in the state of comfort they have already reached. Political is apt to follow on commercial dependency, they say." After a somewhat glowing portrayal of the moral beauty of cosmopolitanism or free trade, Mr. Dilke, recurring to the colonies, says: "On the other hand, it may be argued that if every State consults the good of its own citizens, we shall, by the action of all nations, obtain the desired happiness of the whole world, and this with rapidity, from the reason that every country understands its own interests better than it does those of its neighbor. As a rule, the colonists hold that they should not protect themselves against the sister colonies, but only against the outer world; and while I was in Melbourne an arrangement was made with respect to the border trade between Victoria and New South Wales; but this is at present (1868) the only step that has been taken toward inter-colonial Free Trade."

The British Government cannot, without our consent, maintain its present revenue system for five years more. But we may enable it to postpone the change a few years longer, inasmuch as by maintaining our workshops in England rather than in the United States, we can soothe popular discontent by giving employment to her hundreds of thousands of unemployed workers. This would also not only increase her foreign trade, but by enabling those who are now idle and requiring support to earn wages and purchase supplies, would, till we should again reach bankruptcy, revive her home market.* To repeal or reduce our protective duties, while our people are burdened by the annual levy of more than $100,000,000 of internal taxes, is the only method by which the languishing trade and industry of England can be materially invigorated under her present free trade revenue system.† Should the American people conclude that cheap goods for cash constitute the chief end of men and nations, and that their interests will be best served by having

* See extract from Ryland's *Iron Trade Circular*, in note, page 405.

† See extract from *Our National Resources, and how they are Wasted*, by Wm. Hoyle, page 103.

their ores smelted, and their pig-iron, railroad bars, Bessemer and cast-steel, chemicals, cotton and woolen goods, and other wares and fabrics, made in foreign lands by people whose food is raised by the ill-fed peasants of Russia, Prussia, Austria, and Turkey, the discontented artisans of England will probably be pacified, and the emigration of her skilled workmen to this country be arrested for a decade. What the farmers of the Mississippi Valley would do with their crops meanwhile, is a question worthy of their consideration.

But I may remark that it was the consideration of the question, Where shall the farmers of America find a steady and remunerative market for their crops? that confirmed my adherence to protection. The circumstances were these: In 1859, during the period of doubt heretofore referred to, I sought the privilege of renewing a neglected intimacy with Henry C. Carey, to whom I have since gone, and never in vain, when troubled by doubt on any economic question. Hitherto, our intercourse had been that of earnest adherents of conflicting systems, but henceforth it was to be that of friends in council, or rather of teacher and pupil. I already recognized the fact that with their surplus capital, immense sums of which are invested in our bonds and those of other nations which pay as high rates of interest as we do, it was always possible for English manufacturers, in every department of production, to combine, and by selling their goods, for a season or two, in this one of their many markets, at rates slightly below their actual cost, to destroy their American rivals, whose capital was not often adequate to the demands of their business, and who, when compelled to borrow, were subject to high rates of interest.* And I also knew that the workingmen of this country could not maintain homes and rear and educate families on such wages as those of other countries were compelled to receive. But the question that gave me difficulty was (for such I mistakenly supposed must be a result of protection), why should the farmer be taxed to defend the manufacturer and his employees against such conspiracies, and this inevitable, though fatal, competition? This apparent conflict of interest it was at which I halted, and the service Mr. Carey rendered me was that of showing me that no such conflict existed; but that, on the contrary, the prosperity of the American farmer did then, and always must, depend on the steady employment of the American miner, artisan, and laborer, at such wages as would enable them and their families to be free consumers of the productions of the field, the orchard, and the dairy. With the clear

* See extract from Report of Parliamentary Commission, in note, page 328.

perception of this truth, that, at least in the United States, the prosperity of the farmer is dependent on that of the manufacturer, and the prosperity of the manufacturer equally dependent on that of the farmer; and that, in so far there was no conflict, but an absolute harmony of interests between them, I became a protectionist. My last doubt had been removed, for I now saw that the Protective System was not chargeable with the selfish exclusiveness I had ascribed to it, but was, in fact, the truest and most beneficent cosmopolitanism; nay, more, that it was essential to the enjoyment of absolutely free trade by the American people.

Let me hastily demonstrate the truth of these propositions. Trade is most free when there is an active and remunerative demand for all the commodities that can be produced; and this is when the people are so generally employed in remunerative pursuits that the number steadily increases of those who, by their earnings, can, while supplying themselves and families with the average necessaries and conveniences provided by modern civilization, accumulate sufficient capital to enable them to change their business, or vicinage, as inclination, health, or circumstances may dictate. In other words, trade is most free when the greatest number of people are able to buy or sell, to work or rest, to spend money in travel, or for a coveted luxury—or to deposit the amount required for this in a savings bank, or purchase therewith an interest-bearing bond. The authors from whose works most of the notes by which I have enforced the doctrines of my addresses and letters have been taken, prove that the number of the people of England, Ireland, Scotland, and Wales who enjoy these conditions, is steadily diminishing; that there are more than a million inhabitants of these countries who are vagrants, and more than another million who are paupers; and that this is not because they were born to pauperism and vagrancy, but because, at least in a large majority of cases, they cannot get work whereby they may earn the means of independent subsistence.* As freedom from customs duties does not establish free trade, it has not enabled them to sell or buy freely. On the other hand, the farmers of Minnesota, Iowa, Nebraska, Kansas, Missouri, and Arkansas find that there is such a surplus of food in the world that their trade is greatly restricted. Having all raised grain and live stock, there is no chance for commerce between them, and though we are importing vastly more foreign goods than ever before, they can-

* See statements of Grant, Sullivan, Kirk, Hoyle, R. Dudley Baxter, Smith, and Patterson, in notes, pages 24–5, 195–7, 267–9, 338–9, and 422.

not find a market for their proauctions at prices that will reimburse the cost of production. These States abound in the ores of iron, copper, lead, zinc, nickel, and other metals, and in fuel and water-power. They all raise wool, some of them cotton, and Arkansas is a natural silk field, in every quarter of which the mulberry tree is indigenous; but these exhaustless stores of the elements of wealth, and the forces whereby they may be utilized, have been neglected. Had they been largely appropriated, there would be no glut in the grain markets of these States. Trade throughout their limits would be both free and active. Many of the vagrants and paupers of England have the skill to mine and smelt ores; to convert them into wares; to spin wool, cotton, and silk—weave them into fabrics, and color them with exquisite skill and taste. Can we not, in lieu of homesteads, offer such of their skilled countrymen as still have the ability to come, steady work at such generous wages as will tempt a million or two of them —miners, smelters, engineers, machinists, spinners, weavers, dyers, and other classes of artisans—to come and open the mines of those States, build and work furnaces, forges, rolling-mills, and factories? This would not only give their farmers free trade, but by building up towns, and requiring local railroads, quadruple the price of every acre they own.* This can only be done by putting Protection on the foundation of a settled policy, for who will invest capital in mines, mills, or furnaces to stand idle while we go abroad for our wares and fabrics? Or why should intelligent artisans come here to be idle, or work for such wages as they can earn at home? The farmer should have a liberal price for his grain, but to live well and enjoy free trade he must let others live, not grudging the laborer generous wages for his work, or withholding from enterprise and capital just guarantees of a fair return for their efforts at developing the resources of a new country. Could a million of English people, the adults being, not farmers but miners, smelters, machinists, engine builders, spinners, weavers, dyers, and artisans generally, be induced to settle in the States I have named, and pursue their respective callings, the glut in the grain market would soon disappear, and the freest trade would prevail between them and the farmers. By the pre-emption and homestead laws, we are tempting agricultural immigrants to come by tens of thousands annually to increase our production of grain and live stock. Protection to high wages is needed to bring other classes. The homestead on which nothing marketable can be raised will prove but a poor boon to the

---

* See notes, pages 202 and 360–1.

immigrant. And by promoting the immigration of artisans, we should render to the impoverished masses of England the highest service. By making prosperous American citizens of a million of them, we should improve the chances in life of those who remained behind. The prosperity that would result from the infusion of such an immigration into even the remotely interior States I have named, would quicken the trade of England; for a prosperous people always consume freely, irrespective of the money price of commodities. They will not only satisfy their wants, but gratify their desires; and our importations are always largest when, under protective duties, our labor and machinery are most fully employed. The present is a striking illustration of this fact.

The existing tariff is highly protective. With a larger free list of raw materials than ever before, the rate of duty averages, I believe, about 40 per cent.; yet, our imports are vastly in excess of any former year. How are we to account for this paradox? Thus: We are prosperous, and a prosperous people will gratify their desires. The value of our foreign imports during the last fiscal year was nearly 22 per cent. greater than those of any preceding one. In the year ending June 30th, 1866, they amounted to $444,811,066, but did not attain this magnitude again till that which ended with June, 1871, during which they exceeded it by nearly $100,000,000, having been $541,493,776. This increased importation of foreign goods surprises no intelligent protectionist. It but confirms his theory that protection is the pathway to free trade: that a well protected and generous home market is the only basis on which extended foreign trade can be maintained.* When, as is the case at present, customs duties are so adjusted as to countervail the lower rates of wages and interest prevailing in competing countries, increased importations do not come as they would under free trade, to undermine and destroy our industries, but to supplement them. Our productive power increases more rapidly than our imports, and we are producing each year a greater percentage of our total consumption. But rapid as is the increase of our productive power, such is our general prosperity that our ability to purchase and consume tasks it to its utmost in all departments save that of farming. This is shown by the fact that in those departments in which our production has increased most steadily and rapidly, the home demand is so active and remunerative that it saves us from sending so many of our goods as we did in less prosperous seasons to foreign markets for sale in competition

* See note, page 10.

with the cheaper goods of Germany and England. If readers desire proof that such is the case, they will find it on page 125, of the July number of the *North American Review*, where Mr. Wells enumerates a number of articles of which we export less than we did in 1860, and points to that fact as evidence of declining prosperity. Every reader will recognize the fact that our production of each of the articles named by him has increased in a ratio exceeding that of our increase of population, and see that the circumstance from which the writer cunningly suggests our failing condition, is pregnant proof of our increased prosperity, our power to purchase and consume more than ever before. I may remark, in passing, that this is but a fair illustration of the unscrupulous ingenuity that has characterized the writings of Mr. Wells since his return from England.

Without free access to our markets, England cannot find employment for her people or capital; but as our tariff, by defending the home market, invites enterprise, her capital and people can find profitable employment in developing our resources, and both are coming.* Thus reinforced, we are producing such a proportion of our own wares and fabrics, including those consumed by the cotton planters and tobacco growers of the South, that we can afford to receive in luxuries, or such necessaries as we need in excess of our capacity to produce, part of the proceeds of those special agricultural supplies which Europe takes from us because they cannot be obtained elsewhere. This must be the solution of the paradox, for while augmenting our imports so largely, we are producing not only vastly more iron, steel, lead, copper, zinc, and the infinite variety of utilities into which they may be converted; of cotton, woollen, silk, and flax goods; of chemicals, clocks, watches, jewelry, and works of art, than ever before; but of "dwelling-houses, cooking-stoves, furnaces, pumps, carriages, harnesses, tin-ware, agricultural tools, books, hats, clothing, wheat, flour, cheese, steamboats, cars, locomotives, bricks, coal oil, fire engines, furniture, marble-work, mattresses, printing-presses, wooden-ware, newspapers," and a thousand other things, which, it is falsely said, "cannot be imported to any great extent, under any circumstances," and the production of which gives "to the farmer by far the largest market for his produce." So great indeed is the prosperity of all classes, save those farmers who have gone beyond the reach of a market, that Mr. Atkinson, in his onslaught on Protection in the *Atlantic Monthly*, is constrained to acknowledge that: "At the present time this country is so vigorous, and production so great, that a vicious currency and an enormous tariff simply

* See note from Kirk, page 389.

appear to create uneasiness, but do not seriously impede prosperity."

To have withheld such an admission, damaging as it is to the author's argument, would have been still more damaging. It gives an aspect of fairness and candor to an article that is essentially ingenious and disengenuous; and had it not been made, each intelligent reader would recall the prosperous condition of the country as a sufficient reply to his suggestions: For our general prosperity is not known and felt by ourselves only, but by the British people and government. The Commissioners of Customs state that the amount of the manufactures of Great Britain, taken by the United States during 1870, was £28,335,394, adding that this is "the largest sum ever reached in any year, with the exception of the very prosperous year of 1866, when the values were £28,-499,514, and exceeding the value of the exports of 1860, the year before the American war, by six millions, or nearly 31 per cent." It is not unworthy of note that the only year in which our British imports exceeded those of last year was one of extreme protection, and that in each they exceeded by more than 31 per cent. those of the last year of free trade, or a revenue tariff. A leading English journal, overlooking the fact that the amount had ever been exceeded, says: "The United States have long been the best customers the British manufacturers have had throughout the world, and last year their pre-eminence is more marked than ever."

Thus does current experience attest the mutual dependence of the American farmer and manufacturer, and prove that for them the protective system is the only road to really Free Trade. That at so late a day, as it did, it should have required Mr. Carey to convince me of these truths, illustrates the almost absolute dominion long cherished abstractions obtain over the minds of men; for no fact in our history is established by more abounding proof than the dependence of our farmers on a home market capable of consuming more than 90 per cent. of the annual crop of the country. It is proven anew by each year's experience, and strikingly illustrated by the statistics and general results of each of the alternating periods of Protective and Revenue Tariffs. A thorough examination of these results will, I am persuaded, convince any candid mind that a rigid system of Protection must, for many years, be the paramount political necessity of the farmers of the United States.

But, waiving historical or statistical proof, I propose to test the correctness of this proposition by existing facts. The price of grain is not satisfactory to our farmers, and, as I have more than once suggested, is not sufficient to cover the cost of production and transportation to the seaboard of the crops of the trans-Mississippi States. Is this the result of an unusually fruitful year? By no means. For the yield per acre throughout the country has been considerably below the general average. It is because too large a proportion of our people are engaged in producing grain, and have, in a year in which the foreign demand is exceptionally large, produced it in excess of the world's demand. The leaders of the corn market of England watch the progress of the crops of the Continent as closely as they do those of the British Islands, inasmuch as they usually draw thence from 90 to 95 per cent. of the annual deficiency. And their advices for this year are as follows, as I learn from one of their organs, published September 11th: "The great deficiency in the area under wheat on the Continent (in France and Germany), as reported by us in May last, could not fail to show a very large falling off in their crop as compared with 1868 and 1869, and hence, instead of being liberal exporters of grain as formerly, they will require to import freely during the year. Our late advices from Russia confirm previous estimates in regard to their crops, viz.: that their surplus of wheat will be 10 per cent. less than last year." If, under these circumstances, there be no market for our crop, when and where may we expect to find one? Certainly the near future does not promise a European one; for the war between France and Germany has terminated, and the peasants of both of those countries are preparing their fields for the production of the usual amount of grain for the English market in 1872. Nor is the remoter prospect more promising. The increase of the population of Europe is scarcely appreciable. But her capitalists adopt improved methods of production, and the rapid extension of her railroad system is bringing her interior grain fields into cheaper and more rapid communication with her capitals and seaports. Under these circumstances, to anticipate a steady and remunerative trans-Atlantic market for our grain would be absurd. And what is the outlook at home? For the farmers of the remote interior it is even more gloomy. Our laws offer sublime inducements to the peasantry of the world to come and increase our production of grain. To every one who will do this, they offer with citizenship and free schools a farm without money and without price; and constantly increasing tens of thousands of them are accepting the offer annually. I do not think it would be an exaggeration to place the number of new farms that will be prepared for crops this year, in the six States I have heretofore named, at one hundred thousand. Who are to consume their productions?

Says Professor Kirk, in his admirable essays on "Social

Politics in Great Britain and Ireland:" "There are above 70,000 souls in the east end of London who must emigrate speedily or die. . . . . Above 25,000 of these are workmen more or less skilled in engineer and shipbuilding occupations. These are not shepherds, nor are they ploughmen, nor will they ever be to any great extent one or the other. They are mechanics, and will be so go where they may. In the vast hives of industry in Lancashire there are a greater number who must emigrate or die. . . . . Not one is either pastoral or agricultural, and few are likely ever to be either."

Some of these, he tells, are able to get off "to Massachusetts to find full occupation in cotton." Charity is sending others, and the Government transporting as many as it can to its North American provinces. Can we not prove our cosmopolitanism, and our desire that all men may trade freely, by giving 150,000 skilled workmen of London and Lancashire the guarantee of steady work at generous wages, and so open a way for the employment of those who, for the want of passage money, must otherwise die, as *Blackwood* says, "from sheer famine in the heart of the wealthiest city of the world?" What a market would they and their families create for farm products in all their varieties, and how immensely and rapidly would the application of their skill and industry to our undeveloped resources increase the general wealth of the country!

Let the report of our high wages, *with assurances that these shall be protected by law*, be made in all the great industrial centres of Great Britain, France, Belgium, and Germany, as the freedom of our public lands has been in the pastoral and agricultural districts, and our farmers will not long want a market. But this involves the maintenance of a rigid and generous system of Protection. In the addresses and letters, which compose this volume, the reader will find little else than the application of the principles here enunciated to questions of policy as they have arisen since the suppression of the rebellion.

In advocating such a system of Protection as would enable our miners and manufacturers to pay wages sufficiently liberal to induce skilled workmen to immigrate and enable them to become liberal consumers, I have believed that I was asserting and defending the right of the American farmer to a market—a remunerative market—for his crops. Should this volume convince any number of my countrymen of the correctness of these views, it will vindicate the judgment of those who persuaded me to prepare it for publication, and gratify the most ardent wish of

THE AUTHOR.

PHILADELPHIA,
November 1*st*, 1871.

APPENDIX.

(*Extracts referred to on page* 12.)

LET us for a moment think what are the conditions of our poor to-day. *Apart from the question of our agricultural population, whose almost hopeless lot is best told by the simple fact, that in many places the luxury of meat is comparatively unknown;* apart from the questions of special emergency, such as the cotton famine, or the East End Emigration Society, which has been brought into existence for the purpose of relieving the great mass of destitution and poverty in that neighborhood; apart from all such special and exceptional cases, we have the general sense of depression and want everywhere spread around us. It is not necessary to dwell on the scenes of human misery, where wholesale suicides or cruel murders mark the profound despair of those who lay trembling on the confines of want. It is equally unnecessary to recall those verdicts that appear time after time at coroner's inquests under the simple but expressive phraseology —"Death from Starvation." It is not necessary to recall these things, because the newspaper press of the country drives these truths home without stint and without compromise; but it may be important to remember that the individual cases, which thus come to the surface, are known only by accident, and that the great mass of misery that suffers and dies,—dies and tells no tale. Occasionally and by accident the curtain is drawn on one side, and we see into the midst of the life of poverty that surrounds us; and we then know by the glance thus afforded us, what the general life must be; wasted by poverty, decimated by fever, shattered by want; and it thus rises before us, in the full force of its appeal to that sense of human sympathy which is common to us all. But the general acceptance of the positions here stated will be aided by a few facts. Let us see what the barometer of pauperism has to tell us. Our pauper population in 1866, was 920,344; in 1867, 958,824; in 1868, 1,034,823; and the number is still increasing; yet these numbers show that our pauper population has increased 114,479 persons in two years, or at the rate of more than 1000 per week.—*Home Politics, by Daniel Grant*, p. 3. London, 1870.

We are told that our manufacturing industries, far from being ruined, are prosperous. It is true they are not yet ruined, but many are more depressed than they have ever before been. Very many of them are sick—very sick; far more so than those unacquainted with them have any idea of, and a few years more of such depression will see many of them *in extremis*. There are many who argue that our manufacturers would at once give up manufacturing if it did not pay; and no doubt it is a very natural assumption, that if a manufacturer continues his business it is a proof he is making money by it; but it is very often the case that he continues to manufacture only because he cannot afford to stop. They little know how many manufacturers continue to struggle on in business merely because they do not know how to get out of it. A man with twenty, thirty, fifty, or a hundred thousand pounds sunk in works and machinery cannot give up business without ruin. The causes that diminish the demand for his produce diminish also the value of his plant; his capital and interest are imperilled at the same time and by the same cause. It is not to be expected, it is not in the nature of Englishmen, that he should at once throw up the sponge, and declare himself beat; he will continue to tread the mill though he gets nothing for it; he will struggle on for years, losing steadily, perhaps, but yet hopeful of a change. Millions of manufacturing capital are in that condition in England at present. Capitalists continue to employ their capital in manufacturing industries because it is already invested in them; but in many cases it is earning no profit, and in others diminishing year by year.

It takes some time to scatter the wealth of England. The growth of half a century of industrial success is not kicked over in a day. Moreover, it is only now, only within the last three years, that the foreign producers have acquired the skill and capital and machinery that enable them really to press us out of our own markets. The shadow has been coming over us for many years, but it is only just now we are beginning to feel the substance; their progress corresponds with our decline. A great manufacturing nation like England does not suddenly collapse and give place to another; her industries are slowly, bit by bit, replaced by those of other countries; the process is gradual, and we are undergoing it at present. The difference between England and her young manufacturing rivals is simple, but alarming. France, Austria, Prussia, Belgium, Switzerland, have increased their export trade and their home consumption: England has increased her export trade, but her home consumption has fallen away, in the matter of cotton alone, 35 per cent. in three years!

In the present condition of manufacturing industries it is foolish to tell the operative class to attribute the prosperity to Free Trade; they are not prosperous; it is a mockery to tell them to thank God for a full stomach, when they are empty! they are *not* well off; never has starvation, pauperism, crime, discontent, been so plentiful in the manufacturing districts—never since England has been a manufacturing country has *every* industry great or small been so completely depressed, never has work been so impossible to find, never have the means and savings of the working classes been at so low an ebb.

We have had periods when some two or three of the great industries were depressed, but health still remained in a number of small ones: now the depression is universal; the only industry in the country that is really flourishing is that of the machine makers, turning out spinning and weaving machinery for foreign countries! Many of these works are going night and day.

Now many persons doubt this distress, deny it altogether, and appeal to the Board of Trade returns and to the dicta of certain retired manufacturers, who, having invested the wealth acquired in former years, and being released from the anxieties and dangers of declining trade, can now, without danger, afford to indulge their commercial theories without injuring their pockets.

The manufacturing districts are depressed as they never have been before, and any one who will visit them may see by evidence that cannot lie, by smokeless chimneys, by closed shops, by crowded poorhouses and glutted jails, by crowds of squalid idlers, that the distress is real. Take the one simple fact that the consumption of cotton goods in England has fallen off 35 per cent. in three years Can any fact afford stronger proof of the poverty and depression of our operative classes? Cotton constitutes the greater proportion of the clothing of the lower orders; when, therefore, the consumption of cotton falls away, it is proof positive that the working classes are taking less clothing.—*Sullivan's Protection to Native Industry.* London, 1870. Am. Ed., p. 17.

How effectively the diversification of our industries and the better wages protective duties enable us to pay for labor is doing this, is thus shown by Professor Kirk of Edinburgh. His figures also prove that British emigrants are no longer chiefly agricultural laborers, but skilled atisans. He says:

"So long as there is inhabitable surface on the earth not yet occupied, it is probable we shall have emigration. This abstract thought, however, has very little to do with the actual facts of emigration as it now goes on. It is, as we have seen, a great delusion for men to think that our emigrants are going away from us because there is no room for them in their native land. It is a still greater delusion to imagine that it is a relief to those who remain behind to be quit of those who go. If our readers will give us a little careful attention, we may be able to make the truth clear as to our situation in this important matter.

"In 1815, the total emigration from the United Kingdom was 2081—in 1866, it had risen to 204,882. That is such an increase as may well arrest the attention of all who feel interested in their country. There were higher years than 1866; but these had to do with the gold fever, and need not be taken into account in our present paper. In 1852, for example, the number of emigrants rose to 368,764; but 87,881 of these went to Australia and New Zealand. It is to the steady flow of nearly 200,000 persons a year, as reached from the small beginning—2081 in 1815—that it is interesting to turn attention.

"And yet it is far more interesting to consider the destination of these emigrants. The number from 1815 gives a grand total of 6,106,392 persons, and of these no less than 5,044,809 went to North America. Large as the Australian and New Zealand exodus has been, it had reached only 929,181 in 1866; that is, it had not reached one million when the American had gone beyond five. It is important, too, to notice that by far the largest number of our emigrants to America go to the United States. In 1866, those to the 'colonies' were 13,255, while to the States they reached the high number of 161,000. It is therefore very clear that it is with America we have specially to do in considering the bearings of this vast and growing emigration. The States of America *are not now a new country*. They begin to have all the characteristics of an old established nation, especially in their northern and eastern portions. New England is a well-peopled region of the world; and, to as great an extent as Old England, it may be regarded as a manufacturing country, and certainly not a land remaining to be occupied. An emigration from Britain to these States is not a going forth to subdue the wilds of the earth's surface, but to increase the population of large manufacturing centres.

"This leads us, however, to notice further, the nationality of the emigrants going from us. Up to 1847, the emigration was from Ireland in a very much larger proportion than from the rest of the Empire. During the following eight years the flow from Ireland became comparatively low, though it still keeps up to a high rate. The emigration from Scotland was next in importance to that of Ireland, when the extent of our population is taken into account. England, with six times as many people as Scotland, sent but few emigrants till of late years. The Irish emigration was so great, that in 1851 the census revealed a deficiency in the population amounting to 2,555,720. That is, had Ireland had no emigration in the ten years previous to 1851, she would have had 2,555,720 more than were actually in the island. In 1861, there had been a positive decrease of 751,251, instead of an increase of a much larger figure, and it is anticipated that there will be a still more important decrease in 1871. In 1851, but more so in 1861, Scotland was found to be affected in a somewhat similar way, though not to the extent of producing an actual decrease in the number of people. Instead of an increase of twelve or thirteen per cent., as was in former decades, there was only one of six per cent. from 1851 to 1861. The rate of increase in England and Wales had not been sensibly affected. Now the chief stream of emigration is flowing from England. In the first or winter quarter of the year 1869, the emigration was 2702 Scotch, 9800 Irish, and 11,000 English. It need not be told any one who thinks and reads at all on the subject that it is now in England almost exclusively we have excitement in connection with emigration. And we may assuredly calculate that the census of 1871, and far more fully that of 1881, if matters go on as now, will reveal a decrease in the population south of the Tweed.

"What is the great relation in which these three kingdoms stand to each other and mankind? Ireland is agricultural and pastoral; so is Scotland to a great extent; England is the workshop for these and for the world. There is a small manufacturing power in Ireland, a much greater in Scotland, but by far the greatest of all in England. This explains how emigration did not set in on England or on Scotland, as it has done on Ireland. It also explains why it did not until now affect England as it has affected Scotland. A pastoral people are the first to emigrate in the course of nature. An agricultural people are the next in order. From a land like this a manufacturing people would never emigrate if matters were right. The climate and mineral store of this country are such that no other country can at present compete with it in manufacturing power, if the natural course of things were followed. Even our shepherds have an immense advantage at home, and our farmers have a still greater advantage, but our manufacturers have so great facilities as can scarcely at present be equalled. It is, consequently, matter of extreme interest when we find that

England is emigrating. It introduces us to the mining, mechanical, and manufacturing character of our emigrants now. *There are above 70,000 souls in the east end of London who must emigrate speedily or die.* They are being shipped off as fast as charity and Government can transport them to North America. Above 25,000 of these are workmen more or less skilled in engineer and ship-building occupations. These are not shepherds, nor are they ploughmen, nor will they ever be to any great extent one or the other. They are mechanics, and will be so go where they may. *In the vast hives of industry in Lancashire there are a greater number who must emigrate or die.* These are getting off as fast as they possibly can to Massachusetts to find full occupation in cotton. Not one is either pastoral or agricultural, and few are likely ever to be either. Irishmen and Scotchmen can be anything, but not so Englishmen, and they will not need to be anything in the world but what they have been. Their skill is too valuable to be sent to the backwoods when abundance of rough hands are there already, and skilled men are needed to make a great country fit to manufacture for itself. Till within the last four years our emigrants were chiefly pastoral and agricultural, *now they are chiefly mining, mechanical, and manufacturing.* It is to this that we feel it of such importance to call attention. Our position as a nation depends to a great extent, upon our usefulness to the world in a mechanical and manufacturing line. Commerce has its being in the fact that one nation is so situated that it excels in one thing while another excels in another. It is in the exchange of produce that all trade lies, and such exchange clearly depends on the excelling we have mentioned. If this nation loses its excellence in manufacturing power, it loses its only possible share in the exchange of the world, and its commerce dies.

"We must also look at the effect of emigration on the character of the population left behind. How do the Emigration Commissioners account for the vast deficiencies in the population of Ireland? More than two millions and a half of deficiency was double the emigration, but it was accounted for by the fact that the *young men and women* had gone off to such a degree that marriages and births had fallen off sufficiently to account for all. 'The proportion of persons between the ages of twenty and thirty-five,' in the ordinary settled course of society, is about twenty-five per cent.—that proportion among emigrants is above fifty-two per cent. This is not the only matter of consideration at this point. Miss Rye, in a letter to the *Times*, some months since, said: 'I will not, I dare not, spend my time in passing bad people from one port to another.' And 'bad people' cannot, as a rule, pass themselves; they have generally no inclination to do so. No doubt bad enough people go, but that is not the rule. We dare not now send our criminals abroad, nor dare we send our paupers, nor should we be allowed to send any class unfit to support themselves. *It is the best of our mechanical and manufacturing hands that are now going, and they are leaving the proportion of those who burden society largely increased.*'"—*Kirk: Social Politics in Great Britain and Ireland*, page 112. London and Glasgow, 1870.

www.ingramcontent.com/pod-product-compliance
Lightning Source LLC
LaVergne TN
LVHW011125110826
845150LV00008B/2258
* 9 7 8 1 4 1 8 1 9 4 8 1 9 *